IN 1985 A CATACLYSMIC COINCIDENCE OF PREVI-
OUSLY UNKNOWN PROPORTION EXTINGUISHED
VIRTUALLY ALL FORMS OF LIFE ON THE NORTH
AMERICAN CONTINENT.

ON THE MORNING OF NOVEMBER 29, AN ACCIDENTAL REDUCTION IN POSTAL RATES ON A SUBSTANCE CALLED THIRD- AND FOURTH-CLASS MAIL LITERALLY BURIED THE NORTH AMERICANS UNDER TONS OF BROCHURES, FLIERS, AND SMALL CONTAINERS CALLED *FREE*.

THAT AFTERNOON, IMPURITIES THAT HAD APPARENTLY HUNG UNNOTICED IN THE AIR FOR CENTURIES FINALLY SUCCUMBED TO THE FORCE OF GRAVITY AND COLLAPSED ON WHAT WAS LEFT OF AN ALREADY STUNNED POPULATION.

IN LESS THAN A DAY, THE MOST ADVANCED CIVILIZATION OF THE ANCIENT WORLD HAD PERISHED.

MOTEL OF THE

MYSTERIES

DAVID MACAULAY

HOUGHTON MIFFLIN COMPANY BOSTON

FOR RUTH, WITH LOVE

Special thanks to Nancy Hechinger
and Christopher Davis

BOOKS BY DAVID MACAULAY

CASTLE
CATHEDRAL
CITY
GREAT MOMENTS IN ARCHITECTURE
PYRAMID
UNDERGROUND

Library of Congress Cataloging in Publication Data

Macaulay, David.
 Motel of the mysteries.

 1. Civilization, Modern — 1950–   — Anecdotes,
facetiae, satire, etc. 2. North America — Antiquities —
Anecdotes, facetiae, satire, etc. I. Title.
PN6231.C46M3   818'.5'407   79-14860
ISBN 0-395-28424-4
ISBN 0-395-28425-2 pbk.
Printed in the United States of America

M 10 9 8 7 6 5 4 3

The layers of *pollutantus literati* and *pollutantus gravitas* that covered the continent hardened into rock, and knowledge of the "lost" civilization almost vanished entirely. Interest was revived briefly about six hundred years ago with the discovery of fragments from a series of writings attributed to the late-twentieth-century Franco-Italian traveler Guido Michelin (no relation to the Anglo-Italian traveler Guido Blue). The meaning of the few legible symbols, mostly stars in various groupings, could not be deciphered, and the matter was eventually dropped.

Four hundred years later a young and ambitious archeologist named Currant Bunliffe had a revelation. "The suddenness of the catastrophe," he wrote in one of his notebooks, "combined with the subsequent solidification of the surreptitious substance (*pollutantus aliterati*) has probably preserved, intact, a moment of history." He immediately informed his colleagues at THE UNIVERSITY that he was going to search for fragments of that moment. He was never seen again.

Since 3850 hundreds of scholars and souvenir-hunters have chipped away at the continent's alluring crust. Although North America has not given up her secrets easily, a number of significant discoveries have been made.

Evidence unearthed at several widely scattered sites indicates that the entire continent was covered by a complex network of gray and black stripes. Until the development of high-altitude infrared draftsmanship, the intricacy of this network was unknown. Because the various patterns can only be fully appreciated from the air, the German scholar Heinrich Von Hooligan believes the stripes were planned either as landing strips for extraterrestrial craft or as coded messages from the inhabitants of the continent to their many powerful gods.

Since the discovery of such sites as Monument Row, the majority of scholars have agreed that the colored stripes were in fact ceremonial, or at least processional, highways. The clustering of hundreds of monumental inscriptions mounted on huge poles along both sides of a highway was quite common. Each inscription represented a different religious sect or point of view and was placed as near as possible to heaven — the traditional home of the North American gods. The level of spiritual rivalry becomes dramatically clear when we realize that shortly before the catastrophe some of the inscriptions reached heights of close to one hundred feet above the highway. Von Hooligan claims, and convincingly so, that these tremendous heights prove that the stripes were in fact designed to be used by airborne vehicles.

While this preoccupation with religion was consuming the North Americans and particularly the Yanks, who lived in the area called Usa, a number of scientists in Europe had begun to monitor the dramatic increase in *pollutantus gravitas* above the troubled continent. In an attempt to keep vital trade routes open, they proposed the development of an aircraft that would be able to cut through the increasingly resistant air. The discovery of their flying machine in 3902 at a site in Usa was particularly significant because it showed for the first time just how quickly the density of the *pollutantus gravitas* had increased on that fateful November day almost 2000 years earlier.

One of the most significant monuments erected by the Yanks was the great triumphal arch. Because it was located in the center of Usa, scholars have labeled it an interchangeable gateway to either the east or west. Its geographic placement would have been more accurate had a large portion of the west coast fallen off into the sea as was predicted and in some areas of the country apparently prayed for. Today, kissing the underside of the arch has become a very popular tradition and is believed to bring good luck.

Perhaps the most impressive surviving examples of Yank architecture are the imposing Temples of Bigapple. Nestled in a virtually uninhabited jungle on the continent's east coast, these timeless structures signify at least temporary religious stability and stand as a tribute to the awesome technical skills of the ancients.

In spite of the number of significant clues, however, the picture of these fascinating people remained disturbingly incomplete until forty years ago, when word leaked out of Howard Carson's startling discovery at the Motel of the Mysteries.

Before his forty-second birthday, Howard Carson had accomplished nothing of interest. Of obscure parentage, he spent his first four decades untroubled by public attention. In fact, it was not until the autumn of his life that Carson achieved the unprecedented mediocrity that was to make him, by the time of his death, unique among amateurs.

During his early forties, while rapidly consuming the remnants of a trust fund, Carson's interests were divided between his collection of antique space shuttles and a number of questionable, albeit visionary, experiments relating to increased camel-hump productivity. He must also have had some interest in history, because we know that he possessed at this time a fairly up-to-date translation of the writings of the ancient scholar Hoving and a rather dog-eared facsimile of the *Michelin Fragments,* and that he was a subscriber to the *National Geographic Magazine.*

In 4022 pressure brought on by the anticipated failure of yet another of his experiments led the desperate Carson to seek a change. He entered the 116th Cross-Continental North American Catastrophe Memorial Marathon. Little did he know when he set sail for East Usa what lay in store. Less than a month later, and already well behind the rest of the pack, Carson found himself crossing the great rubble heaps along the perimeter of a deserted excavation site.

The ground below his feet suddenly gave way. He was precipitated headlong downward. When the dust had settled and he had recovered his spectacles, he found himself at the bottom of an ancient shaft, facing the entrance of a long-forgotten tomb. The shaft, probably dug by tomb robbers shortly after the tomb was sealed, had been covered initially by the natural vegetation of the surface. More recently, the whole area had been buried under vast quantities of soil from the adjacent excavation.

Unimpressed and rather annoyed at this inconvenience, Carson's first thought was to call out for assistance, but, before he could utter a sound, light from the shaft caught the area around the handle on the tomb door. Upon closer inspection, he discovered that the sacred seal which was traditionally placed on the door following the burial rites was still in place. Staff artists' reconstructions of similar, but always defiled, tombs that had appeared in his most recent *National Geographic* flooded his mind. Thunderstruck, he realized he was on the threshold of history. His entire body trembled as he contemplated the possible significance of his find. The mysterious burial customs of the late twentieth-century North American were finally (and as it turned out, magnificently) to be revealed.

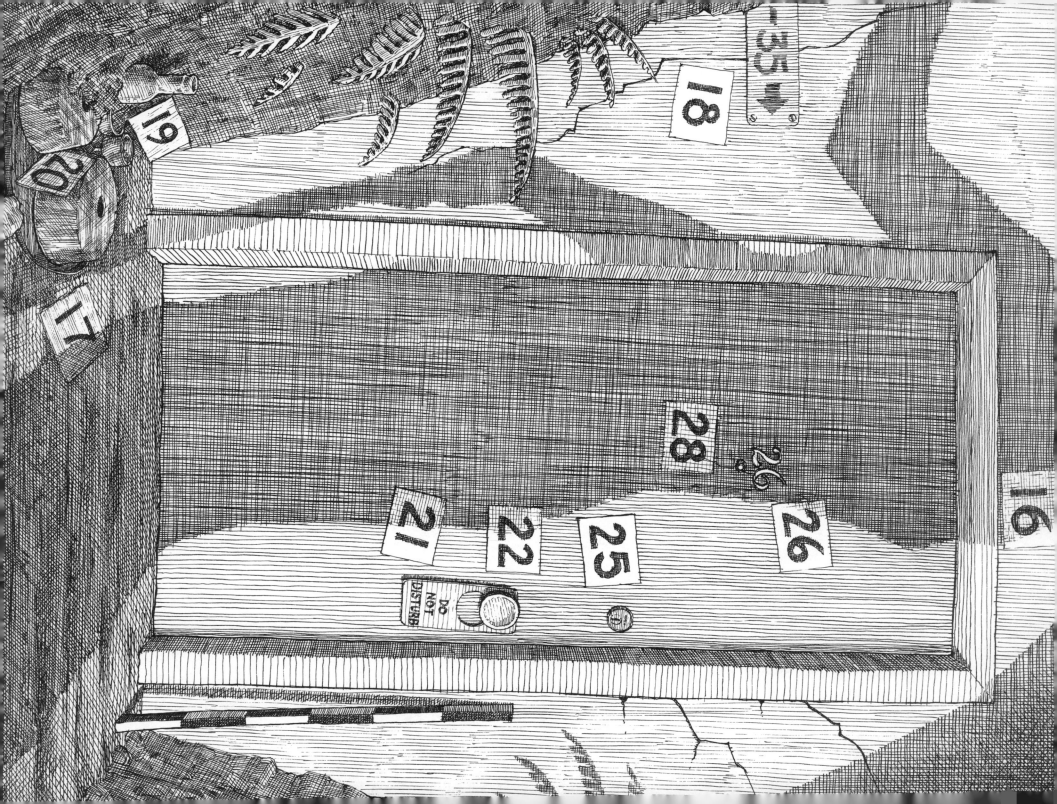

Less than a month later, aided by his companion, Harriet Burton, who "enjoyed sketching," and a dedicated group of volunteers, Carson began the first of seven years' work on the excavation of the Motel of the Mysteries complex, and most specifically on the removal and recording of the treasures from Tomb 26.

While Carson paced back and forth in a supervisory manner, Harriet numbered each of the items surrounding the entrance as well as those on the great door. Descriptions of the most significant discoveries are to be found in her diary:

Number 21, "the gleaming Sacred Seal, which had first caught Howard's attention, was placed on the door by the officials after the burial to protect the tomb and its inhabitant for eternity."

Number 28, "the Sacred Eye, which was believed to ward off evil spirits."

Number 18, "the partially exposed Plant That Would Not Die. One of these exquisite plants, which had apparently been grown in separate pieces and then joined together, was placed on each side of the entrance."

Numbers 19 and 20, "containers in which the sacrificial meal was offered to the gods of eternal life."

Once the exterior of the tomb had been recorded in detail, preparations for entering it were begun. With a steady hand, Carson, who had presumably picked up a few tricks in his time, jimmied the lock. With his helpers peering nervously from a safe distance, he cautiously pried open the door. The creaking of the ancient hinges, in Miss Burton's own words, "cut through the silence like the scream of a ghostly fleeing spirit." Suddenly, to Carson's astonishment, the door stopped dead. A frantic but successful search for the obstruction revealed a beautifully crafted chain about two thirds up the inside of the door, linking it with the sturdy frame. Clearly this stood as the final barrier between the present and the past. Once the workers had sawed through the chain, they withdrew, and Carson continued to open the great door.

At first, everything was dark. Carson lit a match. Still everything was dark. Carson lit two matches. Still, everything was dark. Attempting to avoid a rather protracted delay, Harriet eased the large spotlight toward the entrance with her foot. As the blanket of darkness was stripped away from the treasures within the tomb, Carson's mouth fell open. Everywhere was the glint of plastic. Impatiently, the others waited for a response. "Can you see anything, Howard?" they asked in unison.

"Yes," he replied . . .

"WONDERFUL THINGS!"

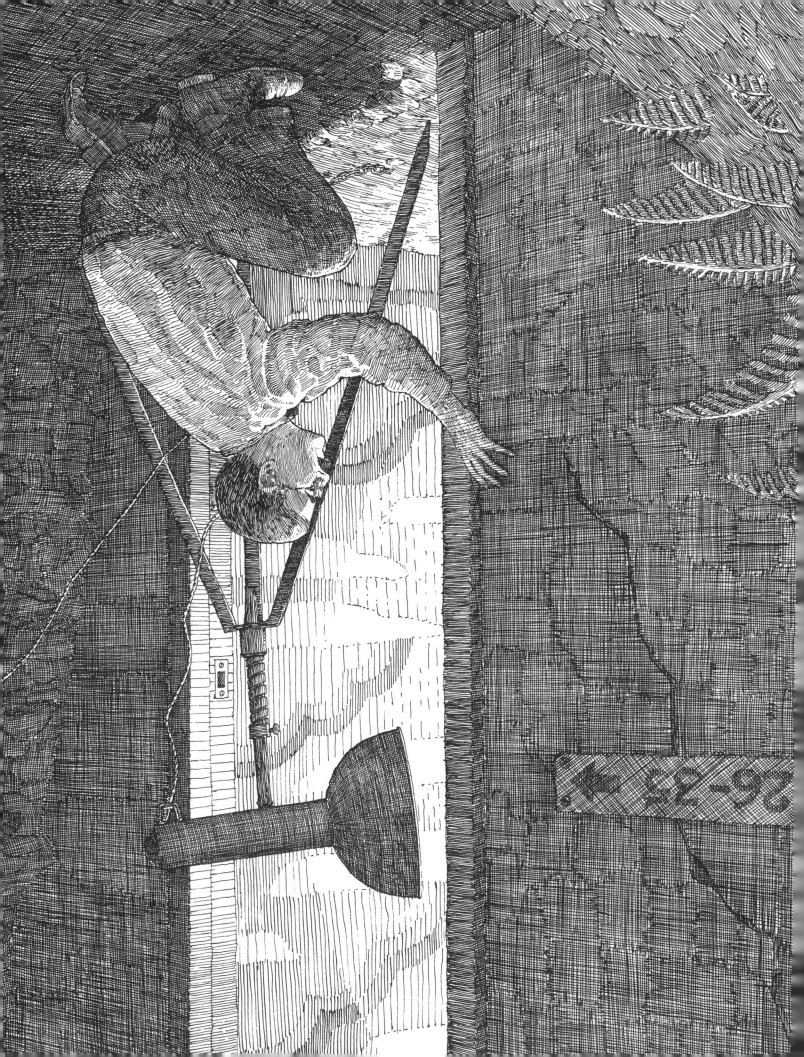

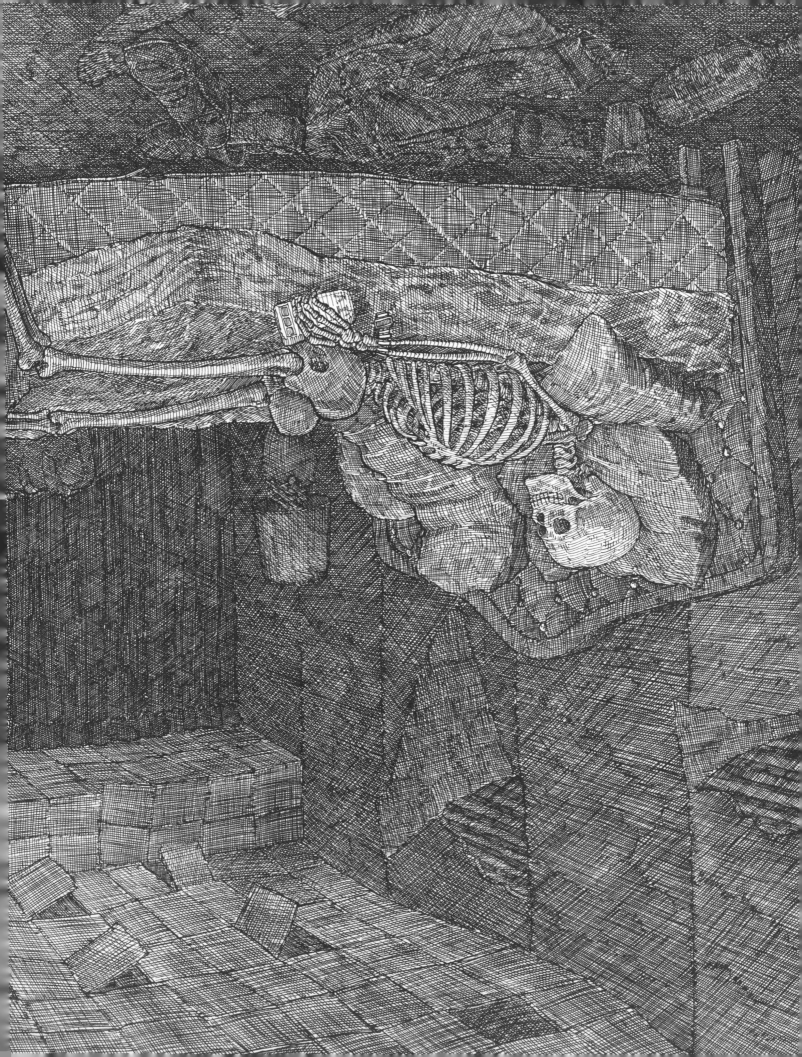

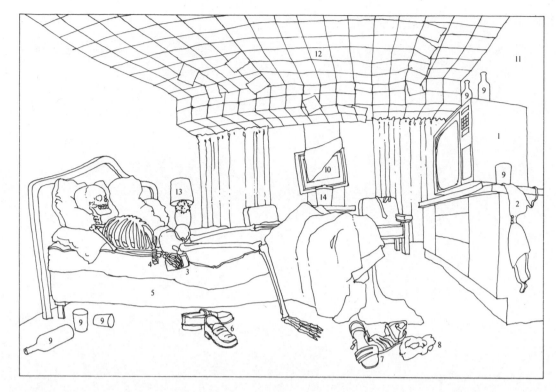

Everything in the Outer Chamber faced the Great Altar(No. 1), including the body of the deceased, which still lay on top of the Ceremonial Platform(No. 5). In its hand was the Sacred Communicator(No. 3) and around its wrist was a flexible golden band(No. 4) bearing an image similar to that of the upper altar. Signs of the ancient burial ritual were everywhere. A variety of garments, including the ceremonial chest plate(No. 2) and shoes designed to hold coins(No. 6), were scattered about the chamber. Various containers(No. 9) which had once held libations and offerings stood on the altar and around the platform. A statue of the deity WATT, who represented eternal companionship and enlightenment, stood faithfully next to the platform. To ensure maximum comfort during eternal life, several pieces of beautifully crafted furniture were placed in the room, along with additional garments stacked carefully in a specially designed rectangular pod. Perhaps the single most important article in the chamber was the ICE(No. 14). This container, whose function evolved from the Canopic jars of earliest times, was designed to preserve, at least symbolically, the major internal organs of the deceased for eternity. The Yanks, who revered long and complex descriptions, called the container an Internal Component Enclosure.

Aware that the two pairs of shoes implied a double burial and having seen only one body, Carson immediately began searching for another chamber. By the time he had found the entrance to what eventually became known as the Inner Chamber, Harriet had already catalogued and numbered it. Quivering with excitement, Carson removed his shirt and began the delicate operation of dismantling the door. Even at the height of his enthusiasm, however, Carson was never too busy to entertain his helpers.

Although it seemed hardly possible, the contents of the Inner Chamber were even more dazzling than those already discovered. Harriet immediately began tagging and identifying each item while Howard drew conclusions. As he had predicted, a second body was present, and this one appeared to have been buried with more care and ritual than the first. Wearing the Ceremonial Head Dress(No. 8), it had been placed in a highly polished white sarcophagus(No. 9), which had in turn been sealed behind an exquisite and elaborately hung translucent curtain(No. 10).

The proportions of the sarcophagus had been precisely determined to prevent the deceased from ever sliding down into a fully reclined position. The similar postures of the two bodies led Carson to the conclusion that the proper burial position had the chin resting as much as possible on the chest. Although the outer surface of the sarcophagus was plain, there were two sets of ceremonial markings on the inside. The first consisted of ten parallel rows of slightly raised discs along the floor of the sarcophagus over which the body had been placed. The second was an almost entirely faded line that ran all the way around the walls parallel to and about ten inches above the floor. Two water trumpets, one about five feet above the other, projected from the end wall facing the deceased. Some of the music required during the final ceremony was produced by forcing water from the sacred spring through the trumpets and out through a small hole in the floor of the sarcophagus. Other music came from the music box(No. 6) situated above the Sacred Urn(No. 2). Articles No. 1 and No. 4 were used in preparing the body for its final journey and No. 5 was the Sacred Parchment, pieces of which were periodically placed in the urn during the ceremony. Carson was overjoyed to find that the Sacred Point was perfectly preserved on the sacred parchment. Very few had previously been uncovered, and none in such remarkable condition. The Head-band, which bore the ceremonial chant, and the Sacred Collar (not numbered) were still in place on the Sacred Urn to which they had been secured following the ceremony.

Gradually, the excitement of those early days gave way to the drudgery of cataloguing and drawing each item in the tomb. Every object was recorded in minute detail in the "appointments" section of Harriet's diary. Those which could withstand movement, and weren't too heavy, were then transported to Carson's rather small but totally inadequate lab for further study and restoration.

The amount of work that had to be done was phenomenal. Driven by an overwhelming sense of responsibility to the past along with a burning desire to contribute significantly to the future, Carson soon lost control of the present. His original schedule of late breakfast, early lunch and tea, and a 3 P.M. picnic at the close of work soon gave way to the frenzied and exhausting pace of an eight-hour day. The strain was to manifest itself in the following ways:

According to Harriet, Carson would often wake up in the middle of the night screaming "Baksheesh" at the top of his lungs. In a recurring nightmare, he believed he was the only human member of a Bactrian acrobatic troupe, and he was always placed on the bottom row when they performed a pyramid. It was also said that during the day, Carson would chat quite freely with either or both of the skeletons, which, in one of his more lucid moments, he had nicknamed Dembones and Dozebones for quicker identification.

In spite of the stories, however, no one had anything but praise for the man's painstaking professionalism. One day, without missing a bite of his lunch, Carson not only brushed each of Dozebones's teeth but also flossed them.

Not surprisingly, Harriet, too, began to feel the strain. In her only recorded outburst, she kicked her way into the lab and insisted that she be allowed to wear some of the priceless treasures. Carson, who was recording what appeared to be impact marks on the top and sides of the altar, realized the urgency of the situation and gave in. For the remainder of the day, Harriet proudly strode around the site wearing the Sacred Collar and matching Headband. She also wore the magnificent *plasticus* ear ornaments and the exquisite silver chain and pendant.

Realizing that Harriet and the volunteers were on the brink of anarchy, Carson called them together and announced he was closing the site for the season. After informing them that he would triple the number of volunteers (by force if necessary) for the next season, he encouraged them to take a long vacation. The offer was gladly accepted by all concerned, and the tomb and lab were locked and barred.

This particular problem never recurred, because with each subsequent season, the number of volunteers increased significantly. Word of the importance of the find had spread around the globe, and eager young archeologists, scientists, and historians flocked to work with the amazing Howard Carson. By the end of the seventh season there were close to nineteen people working on the site at all times. With all the additional help, work on Tomb 26 was completed by the end of the third season and plans were made to begin excavating the surrounding area.

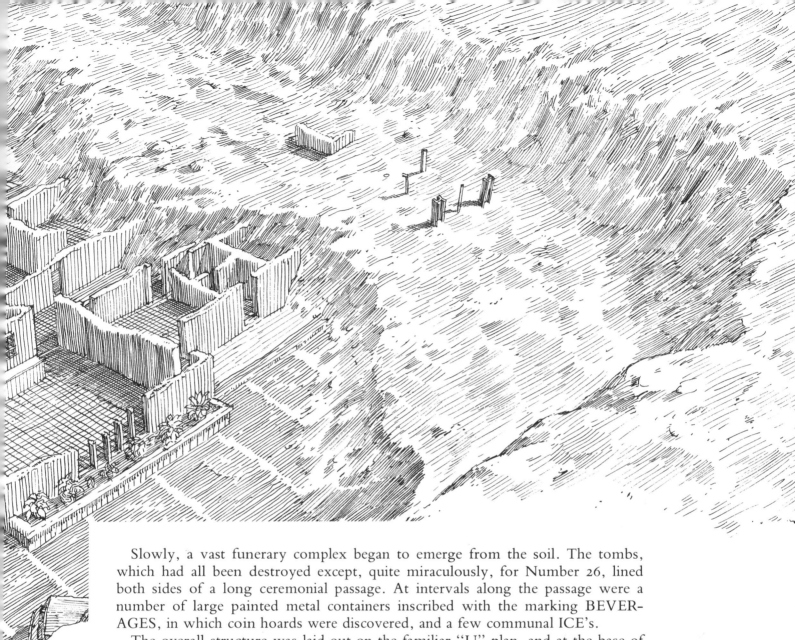

Slowly, a vast funerary complex began to emerge from the soil. The tombs, which had all been destroyed except, quite miraculously, for Number 26, lined both sides of a long ceremonial passage. At intervals along the passage were a number of large painted metal containers inscribed with the marking BEVER-AGES, in which coin hoards were discovered, and a few communal ICE's.

The overall structure was laid out on the familiar "U" plan, and at the base of the "U" was the communal sanctuary. By far the largest and grandest room of the complex, the sanctuary contained a magnificent altar covered entirely in sheets of *plasticus petrificus* or, as it was called by the ancients, "Formica." Behind the altar and mounted on the wall stood a beautifully crafted unit that contained several rows of identical slots, each with a number apparently corresponding to a tomb. Offerings from friends and relatives of the deceased were probably placed in a particular slot once the tomb had been sealed.

Behind the sanctuary was the room in which the sacrificial meals were prepared. Beyond this area was the great courtyard, in the center of which was the ceremonial pool. Prior to the ceremony within the tomb, each body was apparently washed in the pool, which was also fed by the sacred spring. Specially marked funerary game areas intended to occupy the spirits of the dead during eternal life were located around the sacred pool and were accessible to each of the tombs through sliding panels.

Surrounding almost the entire complex was a vast flat area, marked with parallel white lines. In several of the spaces stood freely interpreted metal sculptures of animals. To avoid the misunderstanding that often arises with free interpretation, each sculpture was clearly labeled. They were inscribed with such names as Cougar, Skylark, and Thunderbird, to name but a few. The importance of animal worship in Yank burial customs has never been more clearly illustrated.

Beyond the field of rusting animals, two volunteers began to excavate the Great Sign which had marked the entrance to the tomb complex. Because there were usually hundreds of similar complexes built along both sides of each ceremonial highway, careful marking was essential to avoid incorrect burial.

The accompanying illustration clearly shows that through the years Harriet's devotion to Howard had not waned. His wet but clean bow ties have been lovingly hung out to dry.

Nor had Harriet lost any of her desire to be involved in every aspect of the vast project. When, after years of sensational press coverage, THE MUSEUM finally agreed to show the Treasures from the Motel of the Mysteries in a major exhibition, she worked side by side with Howard to prepare each object for the long journey.

Both Carson and Harriet traveled with the Treasures, although in separate crates, to guard against accident and to reduce expenses. Shunning the reporters and cheering crowds awaiting their arrival, the pair went directly to THE MUSEUM to check a number of last-minute details before the Gala Opening.

While Harriet proofread each of the labels, inserting new words or numbers where she felt them appropriate, Carson inspected all of the reproductions that had been manufactured from Harriet's sketches for THE MUSEUM SHOP. At one point, in order to check the coloring more accurately, he took one of the hand-painted plaster casts of a ceremonial highway fragment outside into the sunlight. This particular fragment had been selected by the TRUSTEES of THE MUSEUM because of its uncanny resemblance to an even more ancient treasure called the Rosetta Stone.

By the time of the opening, there were thousands of excited people lined up under the canopied walkway that surrounded the building — each hoping for at least a glimpse of the treasures about which they had read and heard so much. Aware of the potential popularity of the exhibition and wishing to avoid the congestion that had plagued so many of THE MUSEUM's earlier efforts, the particularly far-sighted Curator of Yankology had arranged the entire display on a specially constructed sloping floor. As the visitors entered the exhibition they were strapped into a pair of well-oiled roller skates.

Carson was so overwhelmed by the enthusiastic response to the objects on display, that he spontaneously removed the Sacred Collar and Ceremonial Head-band from their respective cases, put them on, and performed the ritual chant of the ranking celebrant into the Sacred Urn. Those rolling by at the time went wild with excitement. Swept up in the euphoria of the moment, Carson placed the collar over the delighted Harriet's head, moved in front of the largest spotlight in the gallery, and did what is still believed to be his very best shadow rabbit ever.

Less than a week later, however, the pair were on their way back to the peace and tranquility of the now completely excavated site where it had all begun. Side by side in the twilight, they gazed once again upon the Great Sign. Memories of their initial excitement, seven years earlier, rushed back, sending shivers up and down their spines. Then, as they strolled hand in hand through the glorious remnants of the past, they recalled Carson's fateful fall into the shaft, the almost uncontrollable anticipation at the opening of the outer chamber, and, of course, the discovery of the Sacred Point. They decided that evening that their emotions should be shared with and preserved for as many people as possible. Rejecting the possibility of writing a book — "too static," claimed Harriet — they finally agreed to develop a dramatic living spectacle based on a number of ancient theatrical precedents.

Thus, every summer evening for the past 32 years, hundreds of pilgrims have reverently flocked to the Motel of the Mysteries to witness firsthand the highly inspirational Toot'n'C'mon *Son et Lumière* (French — Mon., Thurs.; Arabic — Tues., Fri.; Hebrew — Wed., Sat.; English matinee — Sun.). At the end of each performance, as the Great Sign fades into the black abyss of night and the orchestral transcription of the sacred chant plays out its final chord, every member of the emotionally drained audience lights the traditional match of tribute. This moving gesture has also been encouraged by practicality, since for dramatic reasons no lights are turned on following the experience.

THE TREASURES

Three Fragments from the Plant That Would Not Die

This plant, developed by the ancients specifically for eternal life, was grown in separate pieces through a now lost biological process. The proportion and size of each plant could then be perfectly matched to its ultimate location. Many such plants were found throughout the complex.

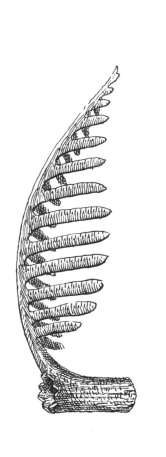
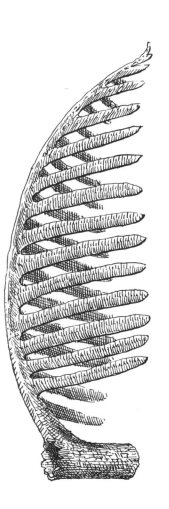
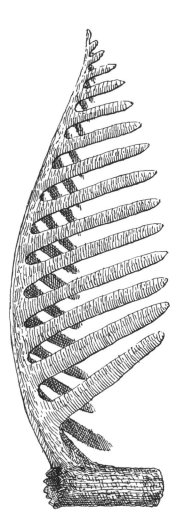

THE SACRED SEAL

Constructed of *plasticus eternicus*, this particular treasure has proportions of classic beauty. It was placed upon the handle of the great outer door by the necropolis officials following the closing of the tomb.

The Great Altar

This magnificent structure, toward which everything in the outer chamber was directed, represents the essence of religious communication as practiced by the ancient North Americans. Although it was capable of communication with a large number of gods, the altar seems to have been intended primarily for communion with the gods MOVIEA and MOVIEB. Judging by impact marks on the top and sides of the upper altar, some aspect of this communication was dependent upon pounding the surface. Communication with the altar was symbolically continued into eternal life by placing the communicator box in the hand of the deceased. Below the exquisite glass face of the upper altar are a number of sealed spaces for offerings.

FRAGMENTS OF *Plasticus Petrificus*

Called simply "Formica" by the ancients (MICA being the god of craftsmanship), these three priceless fragments from the front of the Great Altar represent an unequaled degree of aesthetic sophistication and almost superhuman technical skill. The richness of the coloring and the intricacy of the linear engraving can only be approximated today by using the finest woods.

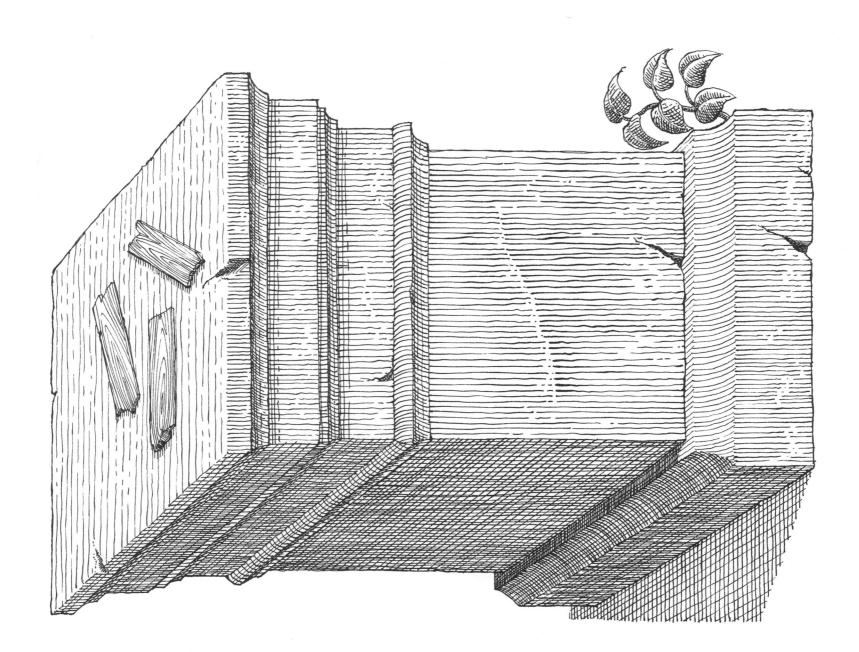

The Bell System

This highly complex percussion instrument was found near the statue of WATT.
Markings similar to those on the face of the upper altar imply a symbolic connection
to the gods. The Bell System was played by holding one half of the instrument in
each hand and banging them together in some pre-established rhythmic pattern.
The impact would cause a small bell inside the larger of the two pieces to ring.
Both halves were connected by a beautifully crafted coil which would miraculously
reform itself into the identical number of loops after each playing.

The Internal Component Enclosure

This exquisitely fashioned container, a twentieth-century adaptation of the ancient Canopic jar, stood on a specially designed table in the outer chamber. The exterior surface of the container was fashioned out of *plasticus petrificus,* while the interior was lined with a priceless translucent substance. Since no trace of an internal organ was found in the ICE its function as a Canopic jar is considered to have been merely symbolic.

SMALL RELIEF

This extremely fine piece of workmanship served as a portable shrine which was to be carried through life and into eternal life. Its delicate inscriptions were intended to identify an individual's religious preference along with the burial site to which the body should be delivered when necessary. Matching inscriptions were found on the main doors of the great sanctuary. Because the ancients were unable to predict the exact time of death, each of the shrines had to last for an entire year.

A Mosaic Tile (restored)

Unlike their predecessors, the ancient North Americans covered the ceilings of their buildings, rather than the floors, with intricate mosaics. Each tile was decorated with a series of parallel perforations, and then color was added by applying the occasional and always subtle watermark.

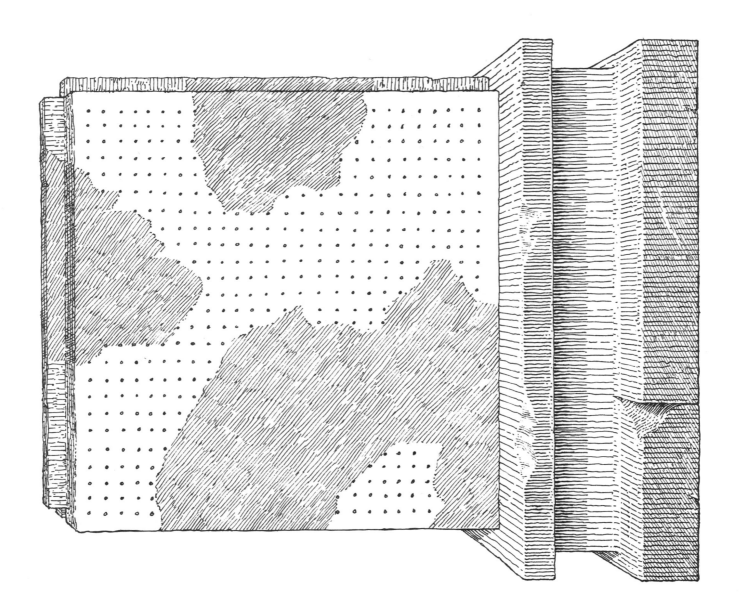

Musical Instruments

The two trumpets on the left were found attached to the wall of the inner chamber at the end of the sarcophagus. They were both coated with a silver substance similar to that used on the ornamental pieces of the metal animals. Music was played by forcing water from the sacred spring through the trumpets under great pressure. Pitch was controlled by a large silver handle marked *HC* (which Carson found particularly meaningful). The instrument on the right is probably of the percussion family, but as yet the method of playing it remains a mystery. It is, however, beautifully crafted of wood and rubber.

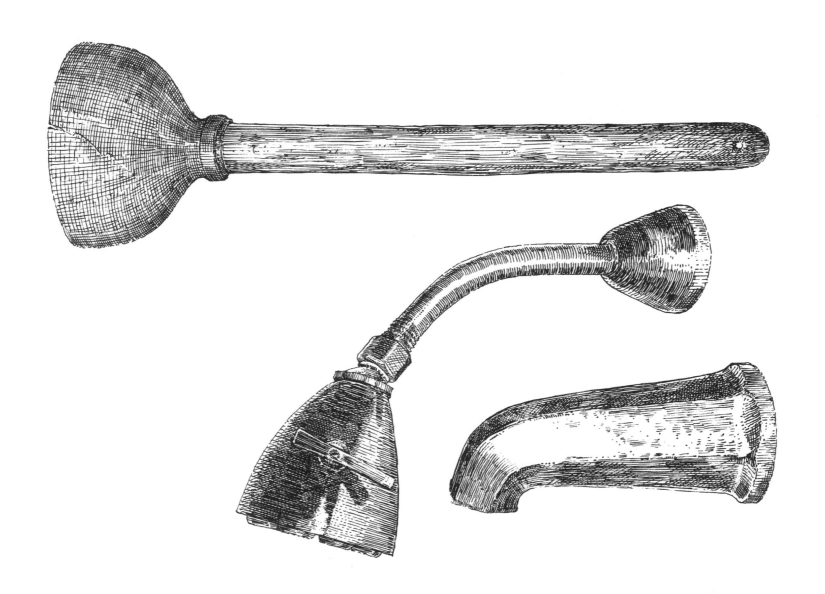

THE SACRED PENDANT

This exquisite piece of jewelry was found lodged in the silver-rimmed hole in the floor of the sarcophagus, where it had apparently been dropped. The beautiful pendant was carved out of rubber (now petrified) and has been inscribed with the markings *1 1/2*. It is connected most delicately by a silver ring to a beautifully formed silver chain. The symbolic derivation of the pendant's form has yet to be determined.

The Ceremonial Burial Cap

This extraordinary headdress, made especially for the deceased, stands to this day as an unparalleled example of flexible *plasticus* workmanship. Each colored disc was applied by hand, and together they form a pattern so complex that a full interpretation of the arrangement continues to elude scholars.

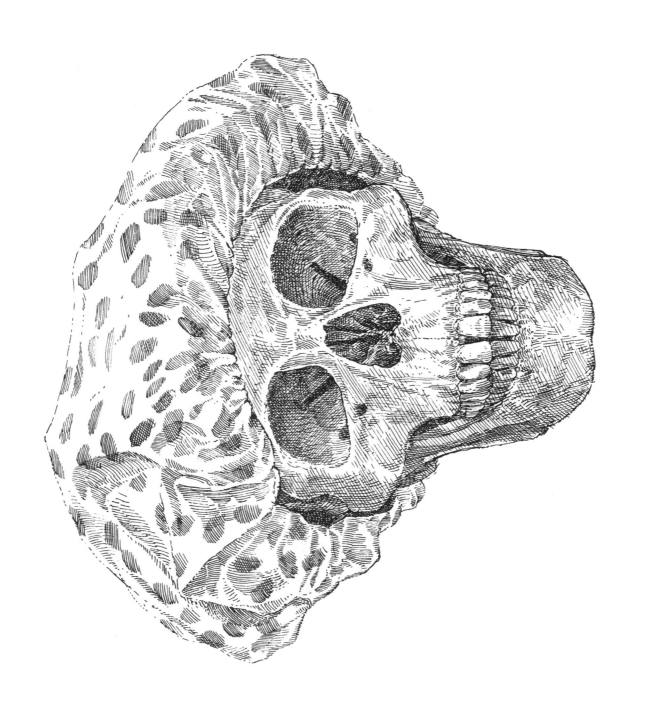

THE SACRED URN

This most holy of relics was discovered in the Inner Chamber. It was carved from a single piece of porcelain and then highly polished. The Urn was the focal point of the burial ceremony. The ranking celebrant, kneeling before the Urn, would chant into it while water from the sacred spring flowed in to mix with sheets of Sacred Parchment.

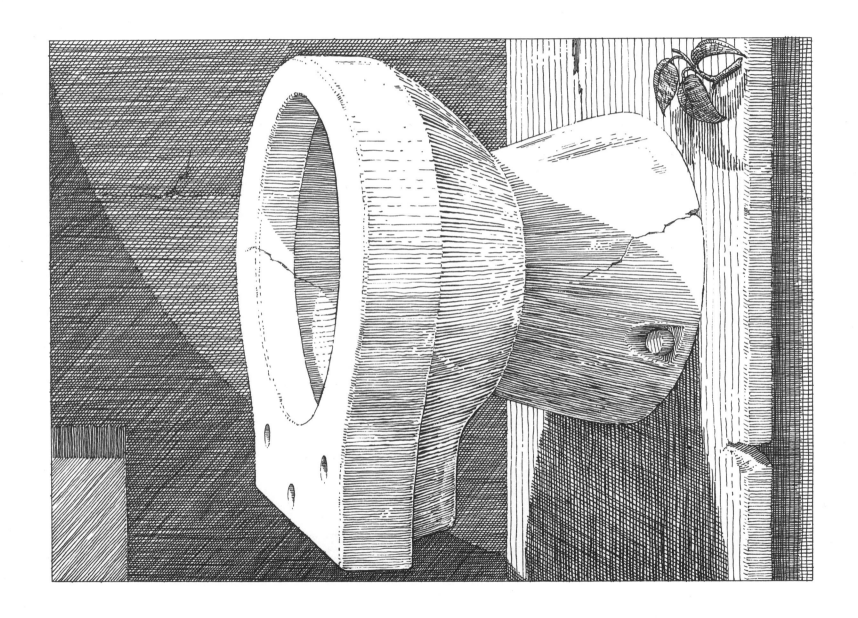

The Sacred Collar

This article was worn by the ranking celebrant at the final burial ceremony. It is made of the highest quality *plasticus,* and the workmanship was unequaled. Experts date this collar at A.D. 1979, making it one of the earliest collars ever found. The two hemispherical projections on the solid portion of the collar were apparently merely decorative. The two spiral connectors shown were used to secure the Collar to the Urn after the ceremony.

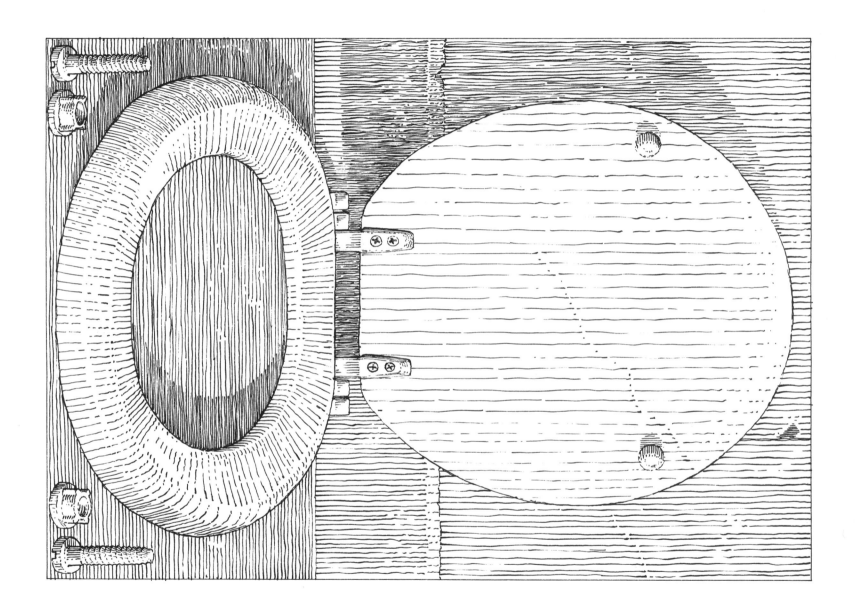

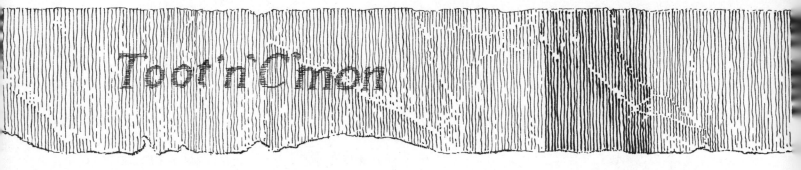

THE SACRED HEADBAND

Another priceless treasure, the Headband was worn primarily to hold the Sacred Collar in place. The inscription on the front of the band is the holy chant. The language was atonal, and the words were pronounced more or less as follows — Sān-i-ti-zĕd fŏřyō-ŭr ṕ-rŏt-ëcti-ŏñ.

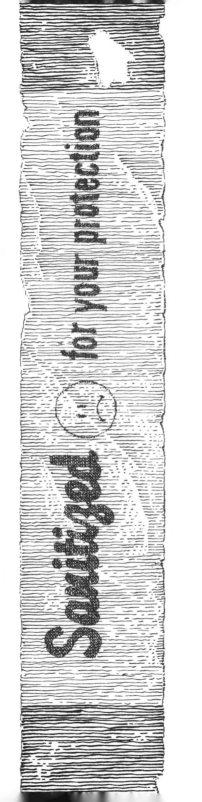

Sanitized for your protection

THE MUSIC BOX

This delicate instrument, placed immediately above the Sacred Urn, served two functions. First, by pulling on the outer handle, the flow of water from the sacred spring into the Urn was begun. Second, once the handle had been pulled, a continuous trickle of water would be maintained by the inner mechanism, creating a simple musical accompaniment which would last for at least the duration of the ceremony, if not well into eternal life.

The Sacred Point

Very little is actually known about the origin of the Sacred Points except that they were very rare and were only ever found on the ends of sacred parchment scrolls. Carson believed that they simply pointed the way to eternal life.

THE SACRED ASPERGILLUM

This beautifully crafted instrument was formed entirely of *plasticus*. Once it had been dipped into the water of the Sacred Urn it was shaken over the deceased and, in fact, over the entire chamber. This represented the symbolic cleansing of the eternal home.

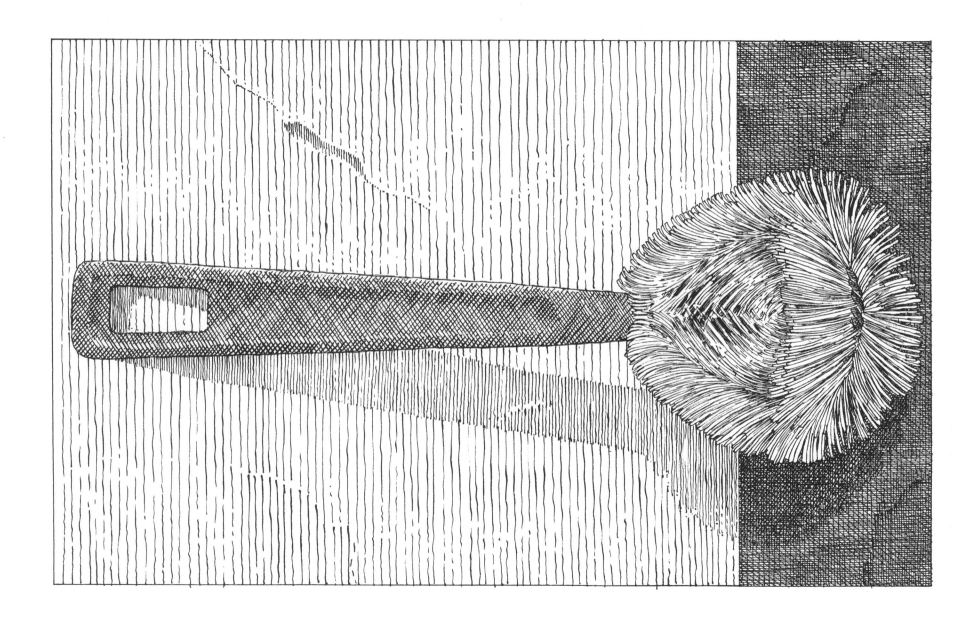

A Yank in the Costume of the Late Twentieth Century

SOUVENIRS
AND
QUALITY
REPRODUCTIONS

Each piece accompanied by descriptive text.

PAPERWEIGHT

Embedded in solid crystal, this pressed reproduction of a Plant That Would Not Die fragment will serve as a conversation piece for years to come. Every mark on the surface of the leaves has been painstakingly copied by our own craftsmen. Each weight comes wrapped in a full-color plan of the Motel of the Mysteries, making it the perfect gift.

SACRED POINT BOOKENDS

Two skillfully reproduced Sacred Points have been mounted on a pair of hand-crafted rosewood bookends, which are then sealed in hand-blown glass sleeves. Your books will never be displayed in greater style. (A set of blank books is also available.)

COASTERS

Each of the seven coasters in this set is based on one of the mosaic ceiling tiles from the outer chamber. The precise markings of the originals have been faithfully reproduced in our own workshop. The coasters, all hand carved in marble, are available only as a set and come handsomely boxed in a 22-karat-gold-over-wood container.

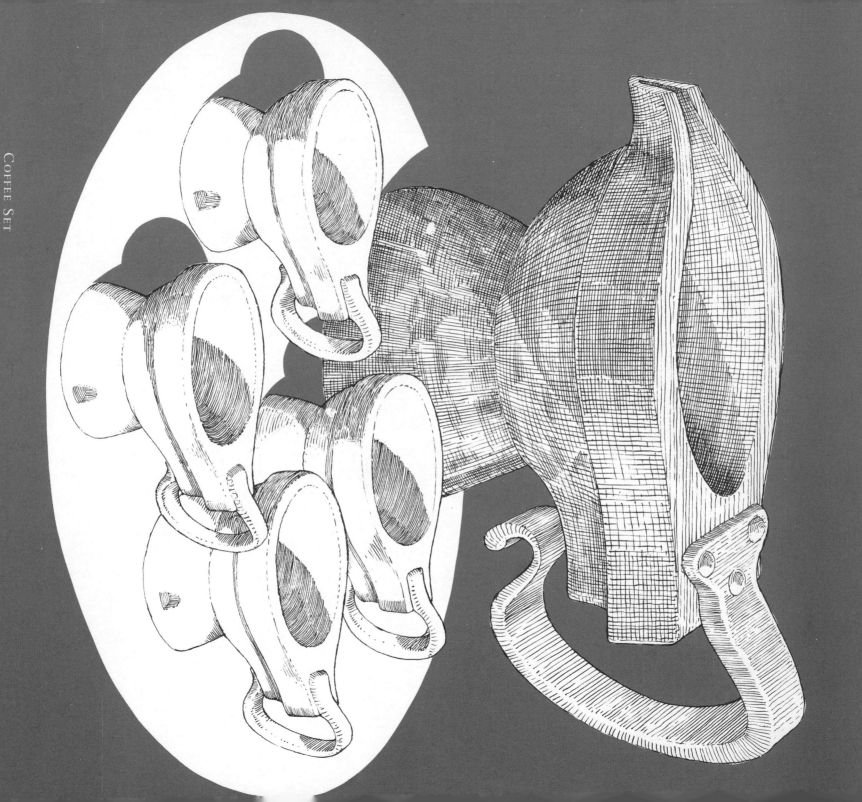

Coffee Set

Perhaps one of the proudest offerings of THE MUSEUM SHOP, this exquisite coffee set is based entirely on the proportions of the Sacred Urn from Tomb 26. The cups are made of the finest porcelain to our exact specifications by a famous English company. The coffee urn is made in our own workshops from solid silver.

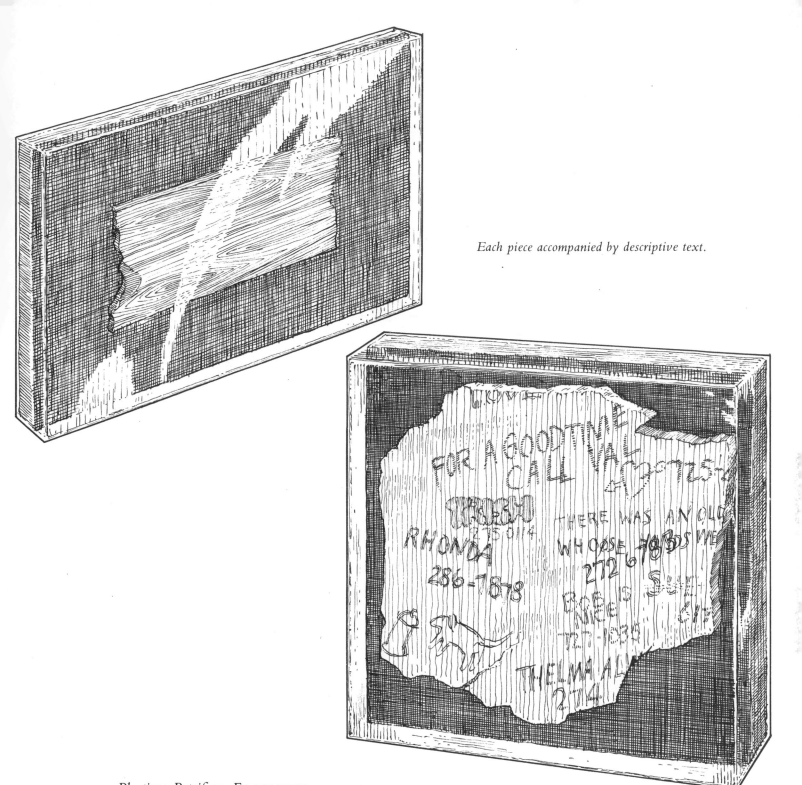

Each piece accompanied by descriptive text.

Plasticus Petrificus FRAGMENT

This beautiful reproduction has been crafted with great care from the finest wood. It is mounted on pure silk and comes either framed or unframed in a crystal box.

WALL FRAGMENT

This unique reproduction will bring culture and character to any room in your house. Based on a fragment found in a multi-Urn enclosure near the Great Sanctuary, each of the markings, believed to be those of laborers, has been exactingly reproduced. This particular reproduction is an extraordinary technical achievement. Because the original was so fragile, it was not possible to make a direct mold. Therefore our craftsmen plotted over five points across the surface of the fragment in order to create an exact-scale model. The reproduction is molded directly from the scale model. The item is available in either alabaster or 24-karat gold.

The Tote'n'C'mon Bag

Designed expressly for the Great Exhibition, this attractive heavy-duty canvas bag is ideal for carrying books and assorted personal effects. Available in tan or gray.

Needlepoint Kit

Based on the stunning frescoes of the Outer Chamber, each kit contains the necessary 13-mesh interlock canvas, colored yarn, velvet, and stuffing to make more than 60 identical cushions for your home and those of your friends.

Mosaic Puzzle

Combining the ceiling mosaic motif of the Outer Chamber with an ancient number game, this engaging puzzle was invented by one of our own guards and is manufactured in THE MUSEUM WORKSHOP. The object is simply to move the tiles around until each of the skillfully reproduced watermarks lines up.

Sacred Seal Belt

This attractive all-leather belt is made especially for THE MUSEUM SHOP by a famous Italian belt maker. The beautiful two-piece buckle is based on the Sacred Seal and the handle from the outer door. Great care has been taken to accurately reproduce the inscription and the proportions of the originals. Both pieces are available in either silver or 24-karat gold.

EPILOGUE

Both Howard Carson and Harriet Burton died tragically shortly after the first performance of the Toot'n'C'mon *Son et Lumière*. Carson was savagely attacked by a rabid dromedary lab assistant when he returned with new hope to his earliest experiments. He passed away just before the birth of the world's first three humper. Harriet was blown from the scaffolding while rewiring part of the huge sound system she had designed for the Toot'n'C'mon *Son*.

Over the years the suddenness of the two deaths has been attributed with growing conviction to the legendary curse surrounding Tomb 26, which supposedly afflicts all those who enter it. A number of additional deaths that reportedly followed visits to the Inner Chamber prompted the Department of Yank Antiquities to order the tomb closed permanently in 4046.